D1453643

Printed in the USA
CPSIA information can be obtained
at www.ICGtesting.com
JSHW081048260524
63600JS00001B/14

"David Shields's genius for deploying the words of others to create wholly original essays is on brilliant display. The connective tissue of his comments is key, guiding us as we jump from Socrates to Luther to Melville to Nietzsche, all the way to Tucker Carlson and Trump. Both erudite and accessible, classical and pop, *How We Got Here* stitches together the threads of thought that have landed us in the nihilistic abyss of today. Illuminating."—Michael Greenberg

"A clutch of intriguing, maddening metaphysical prompts for taking up what Samuel Beckett called 'the old questions' (old, but still waiting for answers)."—Sven Birkerts

"Once again, Shields has deconstructed our collective reality so that we can look at its pieces with the hope that we might put it all back together, a little less slovenly this time. Tracing the path of how we got here is sobering, healing, maddening, and ultimately and absolutely necessary."—Lisa Taddeo

"No barbed wire. No lugubrious ponderosity. Instead, heavy stuff in a light space. Juicy and marvelous."—Padgett Powell

"*How We Got Here* consists of the statements of a culture that has lost its way. The statements are gathered and fed back to us in such a way that we realize—if only for a moment—how our situation became so horribly warped. Where does the truth lie? Work your way through this book and you might just find out."—John Kaag

"*How We Got Here* offers a trail of idea-breadcrumbs through the forest of confusion and viciousness that is current public discourse. By way of apposite quotation and clever juxtapositions, Shields shows us how the human desire to be rational is forever thwarted, perverted, and yet renewed."—Mark Kingwell

Also by David Shields

*Failure Is The Only Subject* (forthcoming in 2025)

*The Very Last Interview*

*The Trouble with Men: Reflections on Sex, Love, Marriage, Porn, and Power*

*Nobody Hates Trump More than Trump: An Intervention*

*Other People: Takes & Mistakes*

*War Is Beautiful: The* New York Times *Pictorial Guide to the Glamour of Armed Conflict*

*That Thing You Do With Your Mouth: The Sexual Autobiography of Samantha Matthews, as Told to David Shields*

*Life Is Short—Art Is Shorter: In Praise of Brevity*, co-editor

*I Think You're Totally Wrong: A Quarrel*, co-author

*Salinger*, co-author

*How Literature Saved My Life*

*Fakes: An Anthology of Pseudo-Interviews, Faux-Lectures, Quasi-Letters, "Found" Texts, and Other Fraudulent Artifacts*, co-editor

*Jeff, One Lonely Guy*, co-author

*The Inevitable: Contemporary Writers Confront Death*, co-editor

*Reality Hunger: A Manifesto*

*The Thing About Life Is That One Day You'll Be Dead*

*Body Politic: The Great American Sports Machine*

*Enough About You: Notes Toward the New Autobiography*

*Baseball Is Just Baseball: The Understated Ichiro*

*Black Planet: Facing Race During an NBA Season*

*Remote: Reflections on Life in the Shadow of Celebrity*

*Handbook for Drowning: A Novel in Stories*

*Dead Languages: A Novel*

*Heroes: A Novel*

David
Shields

# HOW
# WE
# GOT
# HERE

Melville $+$
Nietzsche $\div$
$\sqrt{\text{Bloom}}$ $\times$
Žižek$^2$ $=$
Bannon

sublation
press

Author's note: For the sake of concision, clarity, and stylistic uniformity, I have very lightly edited some of the quotations in this book; I've made every effort to maintain the meaning of the original.

The author would like to express his profound gratitude to Scott Kent Jones, Elizabeth Cooperman, James Nugent, and Doug Lain, without whose invaluable contributions this brief book wouldn't exist.

How We Got Here

First Published by Sublation Media 2024
Commissioned and Edited by Douglas Lain
Copy Editor: Konrad Jandavs

A Sublation Press Book
Published by Sublation Media LLC

Distributed by Ingramspark

www.sublationmedia.com

Print ISBN: 979-8-9901591-3-6
eBook ISBN: 979-8-9901591-4-3

Edited and typeset by Polifolia in Germany

# Contents

## Timeline

I.

1850–1900

Melville, Dostoevsky, Nietzsche:

God is dead, and we have killed him.

II.

1917–1945

WWI and WWII:

Heidegger, Camus, Sartre, et al.:

There is no "essence"; there is only existence—being and then nothingness: only Sisyphus pushing his boulder up and down the mountain until he dies; nothing "matters" absolutely; implicitly, everything is relative.

III.

1950–1970

Derrida, Saussure, Barthes, Foucault, et al.:

Deconstruction: "truth" is dead; explicitly, everything is relative.

IV.

1980–1990

Allan Bloom, William Bennett, Lynne Cheney, Patrick Buchanan, et al.:

Deconstruction, relativism, and poststructuralism are a threat to religion/democracy/America: there are essential truths rooted in the Bible and the US constitution, and we must restore these "truths."

V.

2000–2020

Putin, Surkov, Bolsonaro, Berlusconi, Trump, Bannon, Rove, Xi, Modi, et al.:

The weaponization of deconstruction as political subterfuge: there is no truth; there are only alt-facts; "Democrats" are reduced to trying to pretend that the twentieth century never happened: there are stable truths, etc. The two "sides" have, quite absurdly and impossibly, switched "positions." Giuliani: "Truth isn't truth." *New York Times* ad: "The truth matters."

VI.

2020–2024

The left, traditional media, academics, intellectuals, and "Democrats" finally get it. The authoritarian right has rather brilliantly (consciously? unconsciously?) hijacked the last 175 years of intellectual history and transformed it into hourly political theater. The question becomes: How do we retain Werner Herzog's notion of documentary film as the embodiment of the "ecstatic" rather than the literal truth without also signing on to a completely carnivalesque political life? This book and its companion film are an attempt to trace how we got here and reframe/restart the conversation.

## Preamble: From Ancient Greece to Kierkegaard

*The only true wisdom is in knowing
you know nothing.*
—Socrates

Socrates claimed to be the wisest man in Athens, not because he knew nothing or had no wisdom but because he knew that he knew nothing. Another way to explain what Socrates's claims to ignorance meant is this: those who claim power are ignorant; those who claim power are weak.

Before and during the time of Socrates, seeking knowledge was understood to be the same thing as seeking power. To discover what's right—to know the truth—meant learning the right way to live, which meant knowing how to rule or what should rule your life. The history of reason is also the history of power and of social power.

Plato and Aristotle said, We're done with Ares; we're done with paganism and polytheism; we want a rational foundation.

*If there is some end of the things we
do, which we desire for its own sake,*

> *and if we do not choose everything*
> *for the sake of something else, for at*
> *that rate the process would go on to*
> *infinity, clearly this* [goal] *must be*
> *the good and the chief good. Will not*
> *the knowledge of it, then, have a great*
> *influence on life? Shall we not, like*
> *archers who have a mark to aim at, be*
> *more likely to hit upon what is right?*
> —Aristotle

Thomas Aquinas turned Aristotle, who had been viewed as the great risk to Christianity, into proof of Christianity.

In the time of Aquinas, the Crusades resulted in the recovery of ancient Greek philosophy and literature. For centuries, Aristotle's works had been the bounty of battle and occupation. The Holy Roman Empire absorbed the Greeks; the taking up of Aristotle by the Catholic church was preceded by the spilling of blood.

In his own lifetime, Aquinas was condemned; in the next generation, he was sainted.

In 1274 Aquinas died unexpectedly, and many, including Dante, believed he was poisoned at the request of Charles I, the King of Sicily. In 1277, when Aquinas was posthumously condemned, Pope John XXI was newly elected. The new pope assisted the king in claiming Jerusalem for his kingdom and further assisted him by excommunicating his opponents from the church.

The possibility of Christian atheism began with Martin Luther, who tried to integrate the human and the divine in the figure of Christ.

Luther's Reformation arose when the German princes grew resentful toward the church, especially King Charles V of Spain. The princes wanted to break from the church and establish a German faith, declaring that German money should be for a German church. In 1525, the aristocracy crushed the German peasants' revolt against the Empire; nearly 300,000 peasant farmers were slaughtered. Luther sided with the aristocracy.

Luther's nominalism: nothing exists other than real objects in space and time. There are no universal truths, only particulars.

Nominalism flourished when the church embraced a form of Platonism. For example, the church's doctrine of transubstantiation held that since the Communion wafer and wine were said to be the blood and body of Christ, a process of transformation occurred during the Communion ritual. What had been a wafer and chalice filled with wine are converted by God into the literal blood and body of the savior. However, without a belief in a Platonic realm of universal categories, there's no reason to suppose that some essential property of the wine and bread had to be altered in order for the Communion wine to obtain the property of blood. Instead, the wine is physically wine and is only figuratively the blood of Christ.

What's more significant than the philosophical disagreement that Lutherans had with official Catholic doctrine, however, was that the rejection of Catholic doctrine rested upon the rejection of the church's authority. The acceptance of transubstantiation didn't rest upon theological reasoning; it didn't rest upon the logic of Aristotle or Aquinas; it rested solely upon the authority and power of the Catholic church.

René Descartes enlisted in Prince Maurice's Protestant army during the Thirty-Year War against the Holy Roman Empire. While a soldier in Breda, Descartes studied with the Dutch philosopher Isaac Beckman and was exposed to the leading scientific ideas of the day. He wound up switching sides and joining Maximilian of Bavaria, a Catholic duke.

*Descartes, deciding to work out what he was sure he knew, climbed into a large stove, in order to do so in warmth and solitude. When he emerged, he declared that the only thing he knew was that there was something that was doubting everything.*
—Mike Holderness

Descartes didn't know if he had a body, but he knew he was a thinking substance. He believed he could go from there to proving mathematics and God. I might be in a gaseous cloud. I might be in a computer program. But I'm thinking.

In nineteenth-century Europe, truth, beauty, and goodness formed the holy trinity, science flourished, and Christianity presided over everything.

In 1804, allegedly snatching the actual crown from Pope Pius VII's hands, Napoleon rejected the authority of the pontiff and declared himself Emperor. Napoleon's defeat of Francis II of Austria led to the dissolution of all the hierarchical institutions that, together, comprised the Holy Roman Empire, which ended in 1806. In 1848, Europe was swept up by revolution against monarchical rule and for liberalism and republicanism. In general, Lutherans optimistically welcomed the revolutions.

G.W.F. Hegel's all-encompassing dialectic: Rather than be repelled by contradictions, he located *within* contradiction a spider's web of vibrational spirituality. Everything is always in movement.

In the decades following Hegel's death, a group calling itself the Young Hegelians emerged as political radicals. David Friedrich Strauss, a Hegel scholar and a Protestant theologian, wrote *Life of Jesus, Critically Examined*, which proposes that Jesus was an important person in history but not a supernatural figure. No virgin birth; no walking on water. This historical and materialist understanding defined the Young Hegelians.

The nineteenth century's question: can we get truth without God?

Søren Kierkegaard wanted to find a truth that was true *for him*—the idea for which *he* could live and die.

> *Purity of heart is to will one thing.*
> —Kierkegaard

Kierkegaard: knight of faith, trembling.

When the March Revolution began in Denmark, Kierkegaard was 35. By the time he died in 1885 at 42, Denmark was a constitutional monarchy under King Frederick VII. The constitution established that the Evangelical Lutheran Church was the official Church of Denmark and that all Dutch citizens were free to worship in the manner of their choosing, so long as their faith was not at variance with good morals or the public order.

## Melville

*I hear America singing.*
—Walt Whitman

Socrates and Plato had asked, Can't we do better than Homer? By the time *Moby-Dick* was published in 1851, Herman Melville wanted to return to the Homeric spirit. He wanted to embrace pantheism and be more Ishmael-like: looser, more "irrational" and primitive.

For Melville, there's no difference between the woodcutter, in touch with the god of the forest, and the churchgoer, worshipping the Christian God.

*... each singing what belongs to her ...*
—Whitman

*Melville is worshipping all the gods. He's ready to fast and perform all the rituals of non-monotheism.*
—Hubert Dreyfus

After his father's death in 1832, Melville was employed by his maternal uncle first as a bank clerk and then as a manager of a cap-and-fur store. The Panic of 1837 not only put an end to secure employment for Melville but also drove Whitman's mother's family into bankruptcy.

Ontotheology is a theory of being; Melville would say that the Judeo-Christian tradition doesn't exist, although it's difficult to think of a more spiritually voracious book than *Moby-Dick*.

God is everywhere: God is nowhere? Not quite. Not yet.

*Moby-Dick* is prefaced by "Extracts," fifty pages of completely contradictory quotations about whales. This blizzard of information is dizzying and discomfiting: no one knows anything; the white whale can't be found; your white whale is only *your* white whale.

> *There is no God any more divine than*
> *Yourself.*
> —Whitman

Thirty years before Friedrich Nietzsche, Melville destroyed ontotheology in order to build a new polytheism.

*. . . blood gushing from the whale's heart.*
—Melville

*Whatever satisfies the soul is truth.*
—Whitman

## Dostoevsky

> *It would be a good thing if man*
> *concerned himself more with the*
> *history of his nature than with the*
> *history of his deeds.*
> —Christian Friedrich Hebbel

André Gide described Fyodor Dostoevsky as a genius of the inner world.

> *Nothing is more seductive for man*
> *than his freedom of conscience, but*
> *nothing is a greater cause of suffering.*
> —Dostoevsky

Dostoevsky was an epileptic and gambler who was never not falling in and out of love. When he gambled, he saw Satan; when he didn't gamble, he suffered withdrawal and called on God to save him.

Dostoevsky, a fervent anti-Semite, was obsessed with the late nineteenth-century Russian nihilists, who terrified and thrilled him.

> *It is fifteen centuries since man has*
> *ceased to see signs from heaven.*
> —Dostoevsky

A nervous wreck, a believer, and a rationalist, Dostoevsky asked, If God doesn't exist, is everything permitted?

What will happen to Raskolnikov's soul if he just goes ahead and kills Alyona Ivanova, the sadistic pawnbroker?

> *Oh, ages are yet to come of confusion*
> *of free thought, of science and*
> *cannibalism.*
> —Dostoevsky

Seventy years after Dostoevsky published *The Brothers Karamazov*, William S. Burroughs, returning from a tryst abroad with a boyfriend, "accidentally" killed his wife, Joan Vollmer; he claimed that he was trying to shoot a glass he had asked her to balance on her head during a drunken William Tell reenactment.

What is the "purpose" of our brief stay on earth—simply to experience the widest range of feelings?

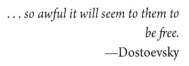

> *. . . so awful it will seem to them to*
> *be free.*
> —Dostoevsky

Eventually, a gambler will lose everything; all gamblers are ineluctably driven to arrive at this moment of dissolution.

> *Only one thing matters: learning to be*
> *the loser.*
> —E.M. Cioran

What happens when you gamble God?

> *Man was created a rebel, and how can*
> *rebels be happy?*
> —Dostoevsky

Dostoevsky's question: Is anybody watching?

## Nietzsche

No one is watching.

In the sixteenth century, Luther got stuck in a lightning storm and wrote a hymn in which Christ suffers in his human nature but not in His divine nature.

> *Luther overcame bondage out of devotion by replacing it with bondage out of conviction. He shattered faith in authority because he restored the authority of faith. He turned priests into laymen because he turned laymen into priests. He freed man from outer religiosity because he made religiosity the inner man. He freed the body from chains because he enchained the heart.*
> —Karl Marx

Three centuries after Luther, Nietzsche said that we took God into the human conversation, into our history, and now He is dead.

God is in human subjectivity, in our bantering back and forth.

In other words, God is nowhere?

Nietzsche's father and grandfather were Lutheran pastors. His father, Ludwig, ran the parish that had been given to him by the King of Prussia, and he was a tutor to the King of Saxony's daughters. In 1848, when the populace demanded universal suffrage, a free press, free assembly, the right to bear arms, a constitutional form of government, and a parliament, Ludwig, initially shocked, took the revolution seriously, although it was soon quashed.

> *In truth, there was only one Christian,*
> *and he died on the cross.*
> —Nietzsche

> *Do we not hear the noise of the grave-*
> *diggers who are burying God?*
> —Nietzsche

> *God remains dead. And we have*
> *killed him.*
> —Nietzsche

—and not so incidentally:

*There are no facts, only interpretations.*
—Nietzsche

*The trust in life is gone; life itself has
become a problem.*
—Nietzsche

Nietzsche thought we were not spiritually mature enough to han-
dle what has come down to us through Western history, and he
predicted the rise of the Last Man.

Thirty years later, Nazism echoed, borrowed from, and (purpose-
ly) distorted Nietzsche.

In late 1944, toward the end of World War II, Theodor Adorno
and Max Horkheimer—German-Jewish, Marxist philosophers—
said that, for Nietzsche, self-overcoming eventually became an attempt to rescue God, who was, after all, dead.

## French Impressionism

In *The Painting of Modern Life* (1999), which examines the political and social meaning of French Impressionism, T.J. Clark acknowledges Meyer Schapiro's 1937 essay "Nature of Abstract Art" as the inspiration for his book:

> *As the contexts of bourgeois sociability shifted from community, family, and church to commercialized or privately improvised forms—the streets, the cafés, and resorts—the resulting consciousness of individualized freedom involved more and more estrangement from older ties, and those imaginative members of the middle class who accepted the norms of freedom—but lacked the means to attain them—were spiritually torn by a sense of isolation in an anonymous, indifferent mass.*
> —Meyer Schapiro

> *I can draw only what I see.*
> —Claude Monet

*Paint objects as they look to you.*
—Monet

*... a bunch of carrots, painted simply,*
*in the personal way one sees it ...*
—Paul Cézanne

*It is only the artists who have taught*
*us the art of looking at ourselves as*
*heroes, simplified and transfigured.*
—Nietzsche

*One sees what one wants to see. It is*
*false, and that falsity is the foundation*
*of art.*
—Edgar Degas

The prostitutes who appear in Degas's canvases—which Paris newspapers treated as spectacle/scandal—transformed his work from an (explicit) artistic experiment into an (implicit) social critique.

*Degas* [paints] *types of a cynical and*
*quasi-bestial truthfulness, bearing all*

*the vices of civilization written in large
letters on their triple layers of makeup.*
—Victor Fournel, *Le Francais*
(1877)

## James

> *Everything we look at disperses and*
> *vanishes.*
> —Cézanne

During a spiritual crisis, American philosopher William James wrote *The Varieties of Religious Experience* (1902). He didn't share Nietzsche's conviction that God is dead per se, but in James's psychological and spiritual distress, in the murkiness brought on by neurasthenia (what he also called "Americanitis"), he examined the rituals beneath all religion: here's the Christian tradition; here's the Jewish tradition; here's the Buddhist tradition.

In *Varieties*, James presents not a metaphysical analysis of religious truth but a pluralistic appreciation of religious experience. He's able to look at how religion actually works, how it functions—as an *operation*.

James doesn't genuflect to Christianity; he doesn't judge Eastern religions; he touches on agnosticism and atheism.

> [Human beings] *are sublime in*
> *having invented God and the soul.*
> —Stéphane Mallarmé

In *Anatomy of Criticism* (1957), Northrop Frye, mapping the four main literary genres, refuses to endorse any one of them and, by implication, deconstructs all of them: this is what comedy looks like; this is what romance looks like; this is what tragedy looks like; this is what epic looks like. In *Varieties*, James is doing something similar: demonstrating (perhaps by accident) that if all religions are possible, then no single religion is true.

*The human brain is a museum of*
*contradictory truths.*
—Remy de Gourmont

## Chesterton

*The Messiah will come only when he is no longer necessary; he will come only on the last day after his arrival; he will come not on the last day but on the very last.*
—Franz Kafka

G.K. Chesterton—a wealthy and obese late-Victorian who despised both capitalism and socialism—didn't fit anywhere. He was a Christian who was also a proto-existentialist.

In *Orthodoxy* (1908), Chesterton says that the center of the Christian cross is a literal collision between two pieces of wood that intersect each other. To Chesterton, the heart of faith is contradiction, which could not be more Kierkegaardian.

Faith is tension: a paradox; it's not simple; it's not a circle.

You're never saved. You're always on a journey. You're always steering into or away from a crash.

For Chesterton, the abyss is everywhere. Asked what's wrong with the world, he said, "I am."

> *Man is an exception, whatever else he is. If it is not true that a divine being fell, then we can only say that one of the animals went entirely off its head.*
> —Chesterton

## Dada and the Surreal

Dadaists and Surrealists understood World War I to be a product of the failure of the bourgeois revolutions of the nineteenth century; Dada and Surrealism were art movements that arose as a reaction to the horrors of the war.

> *The man who cannot visualize a horse*
> *galloping on a tomato is an idiot.*
> —André Breton

> *Everything is incoherent; there is no*
> *logic.*
> —Tzara, *Dada Manifesto*
> (1918)

> *All this twaddle (the existence of God,*
> *atheism, determinism, liberation,*
> *societies, death, etc.) are pieces of a*
> *chess game called language.*
> —Marcel Duchamp

*I detest greasy objectivity and harmony, the science that finds everything in order.*
—Tzara

*I am against systems.*
—Tzara

*Nationalism, in its multifarious guises—from Bonaparte's Caesarism to the gamut of national socialisms— came to the fore as the necessary but increasingly inadequate ideology of the state.*
—Raoul Vaneigem
(1977)

According to Vaneigem, Dada and Surrealism were attempts to break from the illusory myths of the bourgeois epoch. The Dadaists sought the destruction of art and philosophy but not their reinvention.

*Dada means nothing.*
—Tzara

*Duchamp's* Fountain *is widely seen as
an icon of twentieth-century art. The
original, which is lost, consisted of a
standard urinal, signed and dated "R.
Mutt 1917"; for exhibition purposes,
it's usually presented on its back rather
than upright.*
—Tate Modern Gallery

*Possible reality* [is obtained]
*by slightly bending physical and
chemical laws.*
—Duchamp

*Nothing that surrounds us is object;
all is subject.*
—Breton

Breton sought freedom through knowledge of the absolute, re-
solving and reinventing philosophy by discovering what was sur-
real or "super real."

*I'm not sure that I'm not dreaming,
but I know that I'm not mad.*
—Breton

*Construct yourselves.*
—El Lissitzky

*Whether Mr. Mutt with his own
hands made the fountain has no
importance. He CHOSE it. He
took an ordinary article of life and
placed it so that its useful significance
disappeared under the new title and
point of view.*
—Anonymous, "The Richard
Mutt Case"

*Abolish memory. Abolish archaeology.
Abolish the prophets. Abolish the
future. Dada is freedom.*
—Tzara

Asked, as a young man, how to further the evolution of French art,
Camille Pissarro, a lifelong anarchist, said, "Burn down the Louvre."
Later, Pissarro, who supported the Paris Commune of 1871, painted "The Louvre, Morning, Sunlight" and "The Louvre under Snow"
after the commune failed and the French National Guard burned
down the Louvre's library during the defeat of the Communards.

*Every act of creation begins with an
act of destruction.*
—Pablo Picasso

*The interlacing of opposites and
of all contradictions, grotesques,
inconsistencies: LIFE.*
—Tzara

*The purest surrealist act is walking
into a crowd with a loaded gun and
firing into it randomly.*
—Breton

*I could stand in the middle of Fifth
Avenue and shoot somebody and I
wouldn't lose voters.*
—Donald Trump

*There is no ultimate Truth.*
—Tzara

In *The Surrealist Manifesto* (1924), Breton discusses Edgar Allen Poe's "The Mystery of Marie Roget" and claims that Poe's story—rather than demonstrating the power of logic and reason to determine what's true—actually demonstrates that the truth can just as easily be founded upon a fiction as a fact. However, "the search for truth is still the goal."

## High Modernism

*There is no there there.*
—Gertrude Stein
(said in 1937 re Oakland, which 30
years later was the birthplace of the
Black Panthers)

In *Literary Modernism*, Jeffrey Perl's key figures are James Joyce and T.S. Eliot.

Perl is Professor Emeritus of English Literature at Bar-Ilan University in Israel. *Literary Modernism* is based on a series of lectures he gave for The Teaching Company, which produces audio and video lectures—delivered by the world's leading educators—for a general audience.

*Mass culture* is a term that was coined in the nineteenth century. The Industrial Revolution brought many changes, including an increase in literacy rates; printed books became cheaper to produce, and railroads made travel—and the distribution of goods—easier. Today, popular culture is considered to be synonymous with consumer culture, which is distributed digitally. Joyce, a socialist, criticized mass society from the left; Eliot, a royalist, criticized it from the right.

*On or around 1910, human character*
*changed forever.*
—Virginia Woolf

Although Woolf agreed with Arnold Bennett, an Edwardian, that modernist "novels are for the most part clogging our minds," she saw this development as a necessary reflection of human beings becoming less coherent, more inconsistent, more fractured. Woolf had extraordinarily sensitive antennae that registered the shifts in culture and belief: the worship of money and goods; commercials on the wireless and adverts in the Underground; the hoarding and the hoardings; the pre-echo of WWI.

In *Ulysses*, Joyce's anti-epic, Leopold Bloom—a Jew—traverses Dublin on a single day. In the novel's opening scene, Buck Mulligan, shaving with a razor and a crucifix, mocks the liturgy.

To Perl, in Eliot's poem "Sunday Morning Service," the boxer, sitting in a bathtub, is as significant (or insignificant) as anything in Christendom, the entire fresco tradition, any human being anywhere.

In Ernest Hemingway's *The Old Man and the Sea*, Santiago catches a marlin, but sharks eat it, and all he's left with is the fish's skeleton.

*Our nada who art in nada, nada be
thy name thy kingdom nada thy will
be nada in nada as it is in nada. Give
us this nada our daily nada and nada
us our nada as we nada our nadas and
nada us not into nada but deliver us
from nada; pues nada. Hail nothing
full of nothing, nothing is with thee.*
—Hemingway

All the tall timber had fallen; all the verities were over. And how do we build a world out of that?

*human kind / Cannot bear very
much reality.*
—Eliot

You might think that Eliot would view *The Great Gatsby* (1927) as something akin to YA fiction, but in fact he loved it, reread it frequently, and even sent F. Scott Fitzgerald a fan letter. Dr. Eckleburg's eyes—which peer out from a billboard in *Gatsby* and recur throughout the novel—appear to have arisen directly from *The Waste Land* (1922).

*Above the gray land and the spasms
of bleak dust that drift endlessly over
it, you perceive, after a moment, the*

> *eyes of Doctor T.J. Eckleburg. The*
> *eyes of Doctor Eckleburg are blue*
> *and gigantic; their retinas are one*
> *yard high. They look out of no face*
> *but, instead, from a pair of enormous*
> *yellow spectacles that pass over a*
> *nonexistent nose. Evidently, some*
> *wag of an oculist set them there to*
> *fatten his practice in the borough of*
> *Queens and then sank down himself*
> *into eternal silence or forgot them and*
> *moved away.*
> —Fitzgerald

The consumer culture that brought The Teaching Company's Great Courses into existence—the culture that modernism relied upon and disparaged—is the infernal lure that plagues Gatsby.

# Heidegger

*In the face of a god who is absent, we founder.*
—Martin Heidegger

Together, Heidegger and Elfride Petri, a Lutheran, studied the work of Immanuel Kant at the University of Freiburg; later, Heidegger focused on Luther, broke from Catholicism, and married Petri in 1917.

Existentialism's opening act: *Being and Time* (1927). "Reality" for Heidegger was not what "reality" was for Plato and Aristotle. For Heidegger, "reality" = "being" (*Dasein*).

Heidegger observed that as our tools and equipment change, we change: the printing press changed us; the airplane changed us. Being is not so much eternal as temporal, but it moves through human experience at a primal level.

Different histories; different epic narratives: it was one way with Homer; it was another way with Aeschylus; yet another with St. Augustine; and still another with Melville.

> *I am a psychological and historical*
> *structure. Along with existence, I*
> *received a way of existing or a style.*
> —Maurice Merleau-Ponty

In *Being and Time*, Heidegger argues rather persuasively and beautifully that the only thing universal to our experience is death—"being" unto death.

No matter where I live, I'm just a person who walks around, uses tools, has sex, and thinks thoughts, but these activities are all going to come to an end. Wherever I am in the world, it's the same: I'm on this journey from "being" to finitude. The only unity in our experience as humans is finitude.

On May 1, 1933, Heidegger joined the Nazi Party.

In 1934, Adorno fled Germany—first to Oxford, then to New York, then to southern California.

> *When we talk about the finitude*
> *of man, about the "thrownness"*
> *of Dasein, about the blind*
> *contingency and arbitrary character*
> *of Dasein, about the ineluctable*

*and unconditional character of death—even when we repeat the sort of trivialities we find in* Being and Time, *in which Heidegger declares, in vatic tones, that the only thing left when we die is a corpse—it appears as if the problems were already solved just by talking about them. It is rather like the situation in which people throng to public lectures in learned institutions because they imagine that when more or less prominent individuals hold forth about the crisis of culture, something has thereby already been done to resolve this crisis. The crucial mechanism here is that if only people talk long enough about the fact that they have to die and life has no meaning, they would not actually need to die and life would indeed possess a meaning.*
—Adorno
(1960)

*I am moved by fancies that are curled Around these images and cling: The notion of some infinitely gentle, Infinitely suffering thing.*
—Eliot

"Being" itself is fragile.

## Existentialism

*What was Aristotle's life? The answer
lies in a single sentence: "He was born,
he thought, and he died."*
—Heidegger

*Thought is the gateway to despair.*
—Bertrand Russell

*The only serious question is whether to
commit suicide.*
—Albert Camus

*Life seems to be over. And life also
seems like a joke that still goes on
and on.*
—Samuel Beckett

*Human beings can never be fulfilled,
because the will cannot be fulfilled.*
—Arthur Schopenhauer

*One must imagine Sisyphus happy.*
—Camus

*I was always grateful for that*
*humiliating consciousness, and it*
*was always there I huddled, in the*
*innermost place of human frailty and*
*lowliness.*
—Beckett

*All thought of something is at the*
*same time self-consciousness.*
—Merleau-Ponty

*It can never be satisfied, the mind,*
*never.*
—Wallace Stevens

*Everything I know about the world,*
*even through science, I know through*
*a perspective that is my own.*
—Merleau-Ponty

*Man talks about everything, and he talks about everything as though the understanding of everything were all inside him.*
—Antonio Porchia

*I will never know how you see red, and you will never know how I see it.*
—Merleau-Ponty

*Painting is self-discovery. Every good artist paints what he is.*
—Jackson Pollock

*Philosophy is not the reflection of a pre-existing truth but, like art, the act of bringing truth into being.*
—Merleau-Ponty

*Art is polymorphic. A picture appears to each onlooker under a different guise.*
—Georges Braque

*You can't have truth without untruth.*
*How strange that the truth should*
*depend on a gust of wind.*
—Heidegger

*There will be a new form, and this*
*form will be of such a type that*
*it admits the chaos and does not*
*try to say that the chaos is really*
*something else. To find a form that*
*accommodates the mess: that is the*
*task of the artist now.*
—Beckett

*I consider myself successful when I*
*do something that reflects the lack of*
*order I sense.*
—Robert Rauschenberg

*Man is condemned to be free.*
—Jean-Paul Sartre

*Mere anxiety is the source of everything.*
—Heidegger

*Modern man still is anxious and
tempted to surrender his freedom to
dictators of all kinds or to lose it by
transforming himself into a small
cog in the machine, well fed and
well clothed. Not a free man but an
automaton.*
—Erich Fromm
(1941)

Buster Keaton plays The Man in Beckett's *FILM* (1965, 20 minutes, nearly silent), which explores questions of existence and perception—in particular, the predicament of the modern "subject." For the eighteenth-century philosopher George Berkeley, a bishop, "to be is to be perceived"; the all-seeing eye of God makes the world coherent. To Beckett, in *FILM*, the eye, the I, the perceiving subject, sans deity, doesn't create a coherent life for the object of its perception but is an oppressive force that the object seeks to escape. The aim is to become a thing in itself, to break free from the caprice of subjectivity. However, the object *is* the subject. The Man is watching himself.

Adorno said that the catastrophe at the end of *FILM* doesn't correspond to death per se but rather to a death sentence in life—a kind of living death for an ungrounded self. We have now "overcome" this problem by externalizing it. We are our own cameras. We carry electric eyes around with us always. We control our own "objectivity." And yet, of course, with each selfie we take, every moment in which we ignore our actual condition, we reproduce the crisis that Beckett expresses in *FILM*.

## Lévi-Strauss

> *The future is a kind of mirror in which*
> *we can show only ourselves.*
> —Arthur C. Danto

> *The first thing we see as we travel*
> *round the world is our own filth,*
> *thrown into the face of mankind.*
> —Claude Lévi-Strauss

In 1963, Susan Sontag said that ex-Marxists were newly drawn toward Lévi-Strauss, a Marxist, in order to "lay their piety at the altar of the past, since it can't be offered to the future. They have moved not only from optimism to pessimism but from certainty to systematic doubt."

Kurt Gödel's Incompleteness Theorem (1913): Any system of mathematics is necessarily either incomplete or logically inconsistent; there are mathematical truths that can never be proven.

In 1947, studying for his citizenship exam, Gödel reportedly claimed to have found a loophole in the US Constitution that would allow Americans to elect a dictator.

The Observer Effect (1920s): The observer, attempting a measurement, alters what he's measuring.

Heisenberg's Uncertainty Principle (1927): Both the position of a particle and its momentum can't be simultaneously and "accurately" measured; measuring position more precisely means measuring momentum less precisely, and vice versa.

(Heisenberg himself would get confused between the Observer Effect and his own Uncertainty Principle.)

> *Every effort to understand destroys*
> *the object studied in favor of another*
> *object of a different nature.*
> —Lévi-Strauss

> *The subject is nothing other than what*
> *slides in a chain of signifiers.*
> —Jacques Lacan

In 1972, in the middle of a lecture Lacan was giving at the Catholic University of Louvain in Belgium, a young man from the student movement confronted him, pouring a pitcher of water on his notes and saying that Lacan's only aim was to convince the audience to accept a dead life in a society built on spectacle and lies. The student, who encouraged the audience, in that moment, to create a revolution, was escorted out of the auditorium. Lacan finished his lecture and then noted that the student was seeking a new master and would probably find one.

The first sentence of *Tristes Tropiques,* Lévi-Strauss's book about traveling and explorers: "I hate traveling and explorers."

I will, of necessity, bring to bear upon every situation my own skewed, flawed perspective.

## Poststructuralism

*It is through* [the gift of speech]
*that all reality has come to man and*
*through its ongoing action that he*
*sustains reality.*
—Lacan

*One often speaks without seeing,*
*without knowing, without meaning*
*what one says.*
—Jacques Derrida

*Who speaks is not who writes, and*
*who writes is not who is.*
—Roland Barthes

*I'm afraid that if you look at a thing*
*long enough, it loses all its meaning.*
—Andy Warhol

*Being an artist now means to question*
*the nature of art.*
—Joseph Kosuth

*What in the end makes the difference
between a Brillo box and a work
of art consisting of a Brillo box is a
certain theory of art. It is theory that
takes it up into the world of art and
keeps it from collapsing into the real
object that it is.*
—Danto

*The "paradox" is only a conflict
between reality and your feeling of
what reality "ought to be."*
—Richard Feynman

*The frontiers of meaning are always,
momentarily, in a state of collapse and
paradox.*
—Charles Jencks

*I don't know where the artificial stops
and the real starts.*
—Warhol

*All there is at the end is theory, art
having finally become vaporized in
a dazzle of pure thought about itself
and remaining, as it were, solely*

*as the object of its own theoretical
consciousness.*
—Danto

*The man who is born into existence
deals first with language.*
—Lacan

*Language is a skin; I rub my language
against the other.*
—Barthes

*Language promotes communication
and understanding within the group,
but it also accentuates the differences
in traditions and beliefs between
groups; it erects barriers between
tribes, nations, regions, and social
classes. According to Margaret Mead,
among the two million aborigines in
New Guinea, 750 different languages
are spoken in 750 villages, which are
at permanent war with one another.*
—Arthur Koestler

*When two characters or personalities*
*meet, an emotional storm is created.*
—Wilfred Bion

*I am interested in language because it*
*seduces or wounds me.*
—Barthes

Both structuralism and poststructuralism are movements within what is called the "linguistic turn"—a refocusing of philosophy away from the material struggle to change society (Marxism) and toward the relationship between and among morphemes, language users, and the world. According to Cornelius Castoriadis, editor of the periodical *Socialism or Barbarism*, the central tenet of Marxism is that "a theory can't be grasped independently of the historical and social practices which it inspires and initiates, to which it gives rise, in which it prolongs itself, and under cover of which a given practice seeks to justify itself." The social practice that was inspired and justified by the linguistic turn is called "liberalism."

## Foucault

> *We are subject to the production of*
> *truth through power.*
> —Michel Foucault

The panopticon is circular: all the prisoners can see one another, and the prison guard, looking over the parapet, can see all the prisoners. This is not just how many prisons are, in fact, built; for Foucault, this is a precise map of power relations: we're all prisoners and we're all guards.

> *Is it surprising that prisons resemble*
> *factories, schools, barracks, hospitals,*
> *which all resemble prisons?*
> —Foucault

In 1971, Foucault debated Noam Chomsky on Dutch television. Chomsky, in his American way, focused entirely on practical political matters. Foucault's stance was Olympian, dismissive.

> *He struck me as completely amoral.*
> —Chomsky on Foucault

Foucault never pretended to be interested in a solution, not even the sine wave of the Hegelian or Heideggerian dialectic; instead, he more or less luxuriated in the brutal tragedy of the human condition.

> *The body might be considered the*
> *hardware of the complex technical*
> *device that is human thought.*
> —Jean-François Lyotard

Foucault, who died of AIDS, (allegedly) passed on the disease to many of his (unknowing) sexual partners.

> *Utopia of judicial reticence: take*
> *away life but prevent the patient from*
> *feeling it.*
> —Foucault

In 1978–79, Foucault wrote a series of essays endorsing the Iranian revolution:

> *For the people who inhabit this land,*
> *what is the point of searching, even*
> *at the cost of their own lives, for this*
> *thing (whose possibility we have*
> *forgotten since the Renaissance and*

*the great crisis of Christianity)—a*
*political spirituality?*
—Foucault

*The soul is the prison of the body.*
—Foucault

We're back to Nietzsche; to no God judging us; to Kierkegaard, trembling; to Dostoevsky's seizures.

*To be a philosopher is to learn how*
*to die.*
—Cicero

*Dying is nothing; you have to know
how to disappear.*
—Jean Baudrillard

For decades, Baudrillard thought we lived in a "post-historical" world of codes and signs, which were managed by the state and corporate bureaucrats. After 9/11, he claimed that history had "restarted." He saw the terrorist attacks as the realization of all the activity that had been stymied by the hyperreality of a world with no connection to human existence.

*I believe in low lights and trick mirrors.*
—Warhol

In the 1950s, Warhol was employed as a commercial illustrator, drawing shoes.

*The most beautiful thing in Tokyo
is McDonald's. The most beautiful
thing in Stockholm is McDonald's.
The most beautiful thing in Florence*

*is McDonald's. Peking and Moscow*
*don't have anything beautiful yet.*
—Warhol

The Pop Art movement, which Warhol emblematizes, didn't start in the US but in the UK, an island nation that was cut off from the world market and had to ration food and goods well beyond the end of WWII. During this era of privation, the British artist Richard Hamilton would peruse American women's magazines and fantasize about the better life he might enjoy in the newly booming economy on the other side of the Atlantic. Hamilton's first Pop Art work is a collage that is constructed out of advertisements and photographs from these magazines and that depicts the interior of the ideal home—a television set, a vacuum cleaner, and a body-builder wearing a skin-tight swimsuit and carrying a giant Tootsie Pop.

*Theatre is fake: the knife is not real,*
*the blood is not real, and the emotions*
*are not real. Performance is just the*
*opposite: the knife is real, the blood is*
*real, and the emotions are real.*
—Marina Abramović

*My subject is the exploitability of*
*feelings, whoever might be the one*
*exploiting them. It never ends.*
—Rainer Werner Fassbinder

*Multiple descriptions are better than one.*
—Gregory Bateson

*We are actually living in a million parallel realities every single minute.*
—Abramović

[Holocaust denier] *Robert Faurisson said that he would accept the testimony only of someone who had been through the gas chambers.*
—Lyotard

*What has happened to good and evil? Seduction hurls them against each other and unites them in a meaningless spasm.*
—Baudrillard

*One day, there will be a solar explosion, and the sun, the earth, and our thoughts will have been no more than a spasm of energy, an instant of established order, a scratch on the*

*surface of matter in a remote corner of
the cosmos.*
—Lyotard

*The twentieth century was a
psychological age: the self became
privatized, and the public arena
(the crucial realm of political action
on behalf of public good) was left
relatively vacant.*
—Roger Smith
(psychologist)

*We live in a strange time;
extraordinary events keep happening
that undermine the stability of our
world. Yet those in control seem
unable to deal with it. No one has
any vision of a different or a better
kind of future. Over the past forty
years, rather than face up to the real
complexities of the world, politicians,
financiers, and technological utopians
retreated, constructing a simpler
version of the world in order to
hang onto power. As this fake world
grew, all of us went along with it,
because the simplicity was reassuring.
Even those who thought they were
attacking the system (the radicals, the*

*artists, the musicians, and our whole
counterculture) actually became part
of the trickery, because they, too, had
retreated into the make-believe world.
Which is why their opposition has no
effect and nothing ever changes.*
—Adam Curtis
(2016)

*I wonder if art has reached a dead end.*
—Eugène Ionesco

*Let us wage war on totality.*
—Lyotard

*With the destruction of history,
contemporary events themselves retreat
into a remote and fabulous realm
of unverifiable stories, uncheckable
statistics, unlikely explanations, and
untenable reasoning.*
—Guy Debord

Joseph Stalin doctored history books and erased his enemies from photographs. To Debord, in a world without history or memory, there's no need to go back and fix the record. The narrative we live by no longer has to either cohere or be comprehended.

"Never has censorship been more perfect. When the spectacle [of society] stops talking about something for three days, it's as if it didn't exist. The spectacle has gone on to talk about something else, and now that is what exists. The practical consequences are enormous." The disappearance of history is the primary source of the power of the spectacle.

*There is, in fact, no Truth. We are too fragile and volatile for that; we work with too many uncertainties. There is rather the continual shaping of something resembling, poorly, provisionally, "truth."*
—Breyten Breytenbach

*It is conceivable that one day the nation-state may fight for control of information, just as it has battled over territory.*
—Lyotard
(1979)

*Knowledge is and will be produced in order to be sold.*
—Lyotard

*The world is not dialectical. It is
sworn to extremes, not to equilibrium;
sworn to radical antagonism, not to
reconciliation or synthesis. This is also
the principle of evil.*
—Baudrillard

## Allan Bloom

The value of poststructuralism/deconstruction lies in its emphasis upon a multiplicity of perspectives.

Perspectivism (the theory that knowledge of a subject is inevitably partial and limited by the individual perspective from which it is viewed) is a challenge to extant orthodoxy. Everyone's point of view is equally valid (and invalid).

Cf. Diego Velázquez's painting *Las Meninas* (1656).

In the 1980s, deconstruction became a *succès de scandale* in American academia.

Lynne Cheney, William Bennett, Patrick Buchanan, et al.—listening to their children newly discuss such notions as the instability of the text (there goes the Bible) and the death of the author (there goes God)—recoiled or pretended to recoil in horror. Whatever happened to truth?

> *Fathers and mothers have lost the idea*
> *that the highest aspiration they might*

*have for their children is for them
to be wise, as priests, prophets, and
philosophers are wise.*
—Allan Bloom

Bloom, who was published by *National Review* and praised by George Will, denied that he was a conservative (he was, among other things, a gay, Jewish atheist who died in 1992—almost certainly of AIDS). As did Lacan, Debord, and Castoriadis, Bloom studied in Paris with the Hegelian scholar Alexandre Kojève.

*The real community of man, in the
midst of all the self-contradictory
simulacra of community, is the
community of those who seek the truth.*
—Bloom

*Openness used to be the virtue that
permitted us to seek the good by
using reason. It now means accepting
everything and denying reason's power.*
—Bloom

In 1988, in a review-essay entitled "The Paperbacking of the American Mind," Dennis H. Wrong, attempting to explain the massive commercial success of *The Closing of the American Mind* (1987), found more similarities than differences between Bloom's book and left-leaning critiques of America such as Charles Reich's *The Greening of America* (1971) and Christopher Lasch's *The Culture of Narcissism* (1979). "Their complaints about the shallowness and philistinism of American culture are much the same."

> *What was right and true yesterday is wrong and false today. What was immoral and shameful—promiscuity, abortion, euthanasia, suicide—has become progressive and praiseworthy. Nietzsche called it the transvaluation of all values; the old virtues become sins, and the old sins become virtues.*
> —Buchanan

> *It is ironic that anyone who appeals to religious values today runs the risk of being called "divisive" or attacked as an enemy of pluralism.*
> —Bennett

> *We are like ignorant shepherds living on a site where great civilizations once flourished.*
> —Bloom

*Where the purpose of higher education once was to enable the student to find truth, the modern university teaches that there is no truth, only "lifestyle."*
—Bloom

*There is one thing a professor can be absolutely certain of: almost every student entering the university believes, or says he believes, that truth is relative.*
—Bloom

*Our differences go deeper than mere disagreement over propositions. [Others'] concepts strike us as foreign. We do not speak the same moral language.*
—Jeffrey Stout

The right had a Critical Race Theory-like talking point: the academic left is poisoning young minds; there *are* stable truths.

## Culture Wars

*The only thing that's capital-T True is that you get to decide how you're going to try to see [life]. You get to consciously decide what has meaning and what doesn't.*
—David Foster Wallace

*The generation of academics coming into power thinks of the idea of truth as a fantasy, as a delusion, as a tool used by the power structure to keep the rest of us down.*
—Lynne Cheney

*I am a Hegelian. If you have a good theory, forget about the reality.*
—Slavoj Žižek

*We're telling each other things that aren't true in order to make political points, rather than engaging in a real search for what's true, what's accurate.*

*It's irrational, and it has a moral dimension as well.*
—Cheney

*As soon as we renounce illusion, we lose reality itself; the moment we subtract fiction from reality, reality itself loses its discursive-logical consistency.*
—Žižek

*I soon discovered, after I became chairman of the National Endowment for the Humanities, that, for a number of academics, the truth was not merely irrelevant; it no longer existed.*
—Cheney

*Foolish is the confusion spread by* [Adam] *Gopnik and others who are nostalgic for journalism's lost objectivity. Recklessly, even dangerously, they blur the difference between fact and truth and condemn honest, essential analysis as mere opinion.*
—Max Frankel
(*New York Times* executive editor, 1986–1994)

*Every journalist who is not too stupid
or too full of himself to notice what is
going on knows that what he does is
morally indefensible.*
—Janet Malcolm
(1990)

*One of the most interesting places
where I've come across what I call
"postmodern babel" is in journalism.*
—Cheney

*Pop culture, America's most
remarkable invention since the car,
spawned a new information culture.*
–Jonathan Katz
(*Rolling Stone*)

*This is postmodernism—the notion
that there is no truth outside of
ourselves; there is no reality outside of
ourselves. There are only the constructs
that we invent. The notion that truth
is something you invent, rather than
something you discover, is a typically
postmodern approach to the world.*
—Cheney

*In place of the Old News, something dramatic is evolving: a new culture of information, a hybrid New News— dazzling, adolescent, irresponsible, fearless, frightening, and powerful. The New News is part Hollywood film and TV movie, part pop music and pop art, mixed with popular culture and celebrity magazines, tabloid telecasts, cable, and home video.*
—Katz

*Once you say there's no such thing as truth, you have no ground on which to make any other claim.*
—Cheney

*Today's irony ends up saying, "How totally banal of you to ask what I really mean."*
—Wallace

*If there's no truth outside ourselves, neither is there any such thing as falsity; there's just your version and my version, and power alone indicates whose version will prevail.*
—Cheney

*Seeing is no longer believing. The very notion of truth has been put into crisis. In a world bloated with images, we are finally learning that photographs do indeed lie.*
—Barbara Kruger

*There is a cancer eating away at the newspaper business (the cancer of boredom, superficiality, and irrelevance), and radical surgery is needed.*
—Howard Kurtz
(host of *Media Buzz*,
Fox News Channel)

*If you're saying there is no reality outside yourself, then you're saying that other people don't matter as much as you do.*
—Cheney

*It's better to be controversial than ignored.*
—Kurtz

*Ultimately, this is the shift that should worry us. Not the waning of print and the rise of television. Not the triumph of visual imagery over the word. But the victory of the resonance principle over the reality principle, the substitution of an electronic commons for the world we actually have in common: the world where bridges decay, the ozone evaporates, people suffer, and economies collapse.*
—Jay Rosen
(journalism professor)

*It's not a surprise that as this way of thinking* [radical relativism] *becomes so prevalent on college campuses, you begin to see it in those segments of culture where well-educated elites often go—in journalism, in the law, in museums. And once it is sanctified (given permission) by so many areas of our culture, it's not a surprise that you see it spreading out.*
—Cheney

*Break the shackles of mindless objectivity.*
—Kurtz

*If you have two guys on a stage and one guy says, "I have a solution to the Middle East problem," and the other guy falls into the orchestra pit, who do you think is going to be on the evening news?*
—Roger Ailes

In *Manufacturing Consent* (1988), Noam Chomsky and Edwin Herman argue that the power of advertisers is one of the five main filters that transformed the news industry from an institution of civil society—aimed at informing citizens so consumers of news could participate in a democracy—into an industry producing propaganda aimed at creating quiescence.

*Annoy the Media. Re-Elect President Bush.*
—Bumper sticker for Bush Sr.

*Every other network has given all their shows to liberals. We are the balance.*
—Ailes

*We're not programming to conservatives. We're just not eliminating their point of view.*
—Ailes

In the United States, cable television emerged in 1948. In 1952, 14,000 people subscribed to local cable TV; by 1962, nearly a million households did. Deregulation created new investment opportunities and launched nationwide networks. In 1972, HBO, the first pay-TV cable network, was launched. Ted Turner transformed his Atlanta channel, WTBS, into a "superstation," and in 1980 he created CNN; the 24-hour news cycle was now here. After his success with the Fox broadcast network, which he created in 1986, Rupert Murdoch hired Ailes to run Fox News in 1996.

*The universe is nothing but a furtive arrangement of elementary particles, a figure in transition toward chaos. Good, evil, morality, and sentiment are Victorian fictions. All that exists is egotism: cold, intact, and radiant.*
—Michel Houellebecq

*Lacan's definition of human deception: in a universe in which all human beings are looking for the true face beneath the mask, the best way to lead them astray is to wear the mask of truth itself.*
—Žižek

*I want to say one thing to the American people. I want you to listen to me. I'm*

> *going to say this again: I did not have*
> *sexual relations with that woman.*
> —Bill Clinton

> *Man is least himself when he talks in*
> *his own person. Give him a mask, and*
> *he will tell you the truth.*
> —Oscar Wilde

> *I often think that when people talk*
> *about truth, they have this idea that*
> *truth is just sort of handed over to*
> *you on a platter—the truth combo*
> *platter, for instance—but it doesn't*
> *work that way.*
> —Errol Morris

> *The truth will set you free. But not*
> *until it is finished with you.*
> —Wallace

In the film version of *Manufacturing Consent*, Chomsky argues that in order to be truly effective at delivering propaganda and creating a passive, news-consuming public, news organizations should appear to have a liberal bias (and, in fact, should have a slight tendency in that direction). In a media ecosystem in which "journalists" are "liberal," the public can rest assured that it need not go beyond the mainstream in order to develop a "critical" perspective on world events.

*Greetings, conversationalists, across the fruited plain. I'm the most dangerous man in America, executing everything flawlessly with zero mistakes, doing this show with half my brain tied behind my back just to make it fair because I have talent on loan from God.*
—Rush Limbaugh

*I am on the radio for one reason: to attract the largest audience I can and hold it.*
—Limbaugh

*Words mean things.*
—Limbaugh

*There is a God.*
—Limbaugh

Bumper sticker, popular in the early 2000s, achieving exactly the opposite effect of its ostensible purpose: FLUSH RUSH.

## Excess

*In a traditional German toilet, the hole into which shit disappears after you flush is right at the front, so that shit is first laid out for you to sniff and inspect for traces of illness. In the typical French toilet, on the contrary, the hole is at the back, i.e., shit is supposed to disappear as quickly as possible. Finally, the American (Anglo-Saxon) toilet presents a synthesis, a mediation between these opposites: the toilet basin is full of water, so that the shit floats in it, visible, but not to be inspected. It is clear that none of these versions can be accounted for in purely utilitarian terms; each involves a certain ideological perception of how the subject should relate to excrement. Hegel was among the first to see in the geographical triad of Germany, France, and England an expression of three different existential attitudes: reflective thoroughness (German), revolutionary hastiness (French), utilitarian pragmatism (English). In political terms, this triad can be read as German conservatism, French revolutionary radicalism,*

*and English liberalism. The point about toilets is that they enable us not only to discern this triad in the most intimate domain but also to identify its underlying mechanism in the three different attitudes toward excremental excess: an ambiguous, contemplative fascination; a wish to get rid of it as fast as possible; a pragmatic decision to treat it as ordinary and dispose of it in an appropriate way. It is easy for an academic at a roundtable to claim that we live in a post-ideological universe, but the moment he visits the lavatory after the heated discussion, he is again knee-deep in ideology.*
—Žižek

*Who believes what today? I think this is an interesting question—much more complex than it may appear. The first myth to be abandoned is that we live in a cynical era ("nobody has any values") and that there were more traditional times when people relied on some sort of substantial notion of belief. We actually believe more than ever now. The ultimate form of belief is deconstruction. Today, almost nobody dares to say, "I love you." What's the problem? What's this fear? Because when the ancients said directly, "I love you," they meant exactly what we mean; all the distancing qualifications were included. So it's we today who are afraid that if we were to say, "I love you," it would mean too much. We believe in it.*

—Žižek

**Ailes**

> *A liar says what he or she believes*
> *to be false, whereas the bullshitter*
> *says whatever is in their interest,*
> *irrespective of its truth.*
> —Joshua Habgood-Coote

In American academic circles, Perspectivism began as an attempt at inclusion, at pluralism; it had an ethical telos. "Traditionalists," critiquing it, said, You're going way too far with this; if everything is permissible etc.

More or less simultaneously, Trump, Giuliani, Conway, Bannon, Putin, and Vladislav Surkov (performance-artist-turned-Putin-strategist) all learned to make the same move: Well, that's just what *you* say.

Did this feint just sort of seep into the water over a generation or two?

In *On the Genealogy of Morals* (1887), Nietzsche argues that morality is determined not by objective truths but by the interests of the moralizer:

*There's nothing odd about lambs
disliking large birds of prey, but this
is hardly justification for holding
it against them that they carry off
lambs, which ask, "Does this not give
us the right to say, 'These birds of prey
are evil'?" There's nothing intrinsically
wrong with such an argument, though
the large birds of prey will look
quizzically and say, "We have nothing
against these good lambs; in fact, we
love them; nothing tastes better than a
tender lamb."*
—Nietzsche

*Active people don't change the world
profoundly; ideas do. Napoleon is
less important in world history than
Rousseau.*
—Houellebecq

According to the 2019 Showtime miniseries about Ailes, *The Loudest Voice*, in the mid-1990s key Fox executives said to Rupert Murdoch that the *New York Times* and the "major" networks all had the same "facts"; let's do something like *A Current Affair* "but edgier." Ailes said, That seems incredibly dumb to me, because half of America doesn't have a voice; let's provide them with a conservative, pro-American message on their own channel. The birth of Fox News.

[The courts and the media elite]
*are abolishing America; they are*
*deconstructing our country; they have*
*dethroned our God.*
—Buchanan

*Once again the powers of light and*
*good have triumphed over the media.*
—Karl Rove
(2000)

*Is it that you hate this president or you*
*hate America?*
—Sean Hannity
(2004)

[The founders] *figured that if*
*everybody got to say whatever they*
*wanted, the people could choose, and*
*the truth would come out in the end.*
—Howard Troxler
(former *Tampa Bay Times*
columnist)

*Bill Moyers, who runs a foundation*
*that funds far-left organizations, hides*
*behind the label of objectivity on PBS;*

*he's about as objective as Mao Zedong.*
*I mean, the guy's a joke. Get out of the*
*news business, Bill.*
—Bill O'Reilly

In 2004, Dick Cheney warned that a vote for John Kerry was tantamount to a vote for a second and more devastating attack from Islamic terrorists. Trump's response: "Well, it's a terrible statement—unless he gets away with it."

*Art is anything you can get away with.*
—Warhol

*Art is heading in no direction to*
*speak of.*
—Danto

*If they wanna be nonbelievers, I don't*
*care; that's up to them. But it's just as*
*much of a stretch to be an atheist as*
*it is to believe in God, because there's*
*no explanation for how the planet got*
*here, and he* [Stephen Hawking]
*doesn't have it, either.*
—O'Reilly

*Life would be tragic if it weren't funny.*
—Hawking

*It's no longer possible to assume any
principle of truth, or causality, or
discursive norm. We must grant both
the poetic singularity of events and the
radical uncertainty of events.*
—Baudrillard

*Our culture is obsessed with "real"
events because we experience hardly any.*
—Andrew O'Hehir
(*Salon* executive editor)

*I believe that we face incredible
obstacles in our attempts to see the
world. Everything in our nature
tries to deny the world around us, to
refabricate it in our own image, to
reinvent it for our own benefit.*
—Errol Morris

Everybody has biases, but some people used to want to wrestle with their own biases as an important part of their investigation of the material. Do people still do this, or does that now feel old-fashioned, even trite?

In 2017, Fox changed its motto from "Fair and Balanced" to "Most Watched, Most Trusted." "Fair and balanced" had served its purpose (gaslighting). Nothing in life is fair; nothing is balanced.

> *God, expelling Adam and Eve, felt bad. You know how you get angry and say to yourself, "Maybe I overreacted"? God thought, "I know: I'll give them self-deception. Things are going to be truly horrendous out there, but they'll never notice."*
> —Morris

Before running Fox News, Ailes was hired away from *The Mike Douglas Show* to become "executive producer for television" for Richard Nixon's 1968 presidential campaign. Would Ailes have read Baudrillard? No. He didn't need to. He already knew all that.

To paraphrase the English mathematician Oliver Heaviside, You don't need a theory of dinner; sooner or later, you're going to find the food you need.

> *Adam ate the apple, and our teeth still ache.*
> —Hungarian proverb

*The fights you have are never about the thing you're fighting about. It's always about something else. It's about a story. It's about respect. It's about recognition, something deep.*
—Barack Obama

*What we can tell you with certainty is that Barack Obama has deep emotional ties to Islam.*
—O'Reilly

*Journalism died in 2008.*
—Hannity

*America today is a confused society—caught up in a terror war, a culture war, and a media war—in which honesty and professional standards have vanished.*
—O'Reilly

*The US is the greatest, best country God has ever given man on the face of the Earth.*
—Hannity

*Here you are: You're a liberal. You probably define peace as the absence of conflict. I define peace as the ability to defend yourself and blow your enemy into smithereens.*
—Hannity

*We're an empire now, and when we act, we create our own reality. And while you're studying that reality—judiciously, as you will—we'll act again, creating new realities, which you can study, too, and that's how things will sort out. We're history's actors, and you, all of you, will be left to just study what we do.*
—Rove
("allegedly")

*[Postmodernism] is a sort of Pandora's Box. It's about color and ornament and triumph.*
—Sir Terry Farrell
(British architect)

*Sometimes compromise is the right answer, but often compromise is the*

*equivalent of defeat, and I don't like*
*being defeated.*
—Trump

*I understand only friendship or*
*scorched earth.*
—Ailes

[The ACLU is] *the most dangerous*
*organization in the United States of*
*America right now. There's nobody*
*else even close. They're like second next*
*to Al Qaeda.*
—O'Reilly

*I don't see any difference between*
[Arianna] *Huffington and the Nazis.*
—O'Reilly

*I'm a journalist, but I'm an advocacy*
*journalist or an opinion journalist.*
—Hannity

*In our culture, we think meanings*
*come from our own autonomous*

*choices and from the force of our*
*individual will.*
—Sean Kelly

*CNN is fake news. I don't take*
*questions from CNN.*
—Trump

[Democrats are] *the party of*
*intolerance, smears, lies, character*
*assassination, besmirchment, and fake*
*Russian dossiers.*
—Hannity

*A simple man tells the truth.*
—O'Reilly

Everyone is biased except us; we're the truth; we know how our base thinks; they'll trust us; and we'll trust them (to trust us).

On January 6, 2017, Jeh Johnson, the director of the Department of Homeland Security, declared that the communications infra-structure of the United States was now under the jurisdiction of his department. In response to Russian interference in the 2016 election, DHS would commit itself to a society-wide war on disinformation. Within DHS, the Cybersecurity and Infrastructure Security Agency (CISA) was tasked with combating disinformation online.

Johnson: "I have determined that election infrastructure in this country should be designated as a subsector of the existing Government Facilities critical infrastructure sector. Given the vital role that elections play in this country, it's clear that certain systems and assets of election infrastructure meet the definition of critical infrastructure, in fact and in law." Johnson listed sixteen "critical infrastructure sectors," including "Communications." In 2021, DHS released a report entitled "Combating Targeted Disinformation Campaigns," which argues that the problem of disinformation would require a public-private partnership to defeat.

In 2017, DHS granted itself the right to determine what was true and what was false, including the right to censor what it determined to be true if what was true might lead people to the wrong conclusions. DHS labeled true but misleading stories "malinformation."

On March 6, 2023, Andrew Bailey, the attorney general of the state of Missouri, sued the Biden Administration, DHS, the FBI, the CDC, and other federal agencies, "to protect the constitutional liberties of all Americans." After examining evidence of censorship by the Biden White House and DHS, the United States District Court for the Western District of Louisiana issued a preliminary injunction against the government and prohibited the government from further acts of censorship.

*One may dream of a culture in which*
*someone says, "This is true," and*
*everyone bursts into laughter.*
—Baudrillard

## The Last Man

Ron Rosenbaum asked Errol Morris, "Are you able to tell when you're deceiving yourself?" Morris's response: "Probably not. There's a certain suspicion I have about people who claim absolute knowledge of any kind, including knowledge of themselves."

Thinking: the surest way to nihilism.

> *The threat of nihilism is a threat that's*
> *peculiar to* [our] *age.*
> —Kelly

> *I shop therefore I am.*
> —Kruger

> *It depends on what the meaning of*
> *"is" is.*
> —Clinton

In 1995, after Lynne Cheney gave a lecture in Boston at Northeastern University, an audience member asked her, "To the extent that [radical relativism] might become predominant, do you see any danger that it would lead to the kind of cynical exercise of raw power that its proponents really abhor? I have in mind the former Soviet Union, where I understand that truth was really that which best served the state." Cheney replied, "I begin each of the chapters of my book [*Telling the Truth*] with a quotation from George Orwell. I did this in part because Orwell was a socialist, and I wanted to make the point that this is not something that only conservatives worry about. This is something for us all to worry about. Many of the quotes are from *1984*, which was, at least in part, Orwell's take on the Soviet Union. I had a chance to visit the Soviet Union the year after the Berlin Wall came down and the empire began to disintegrate. One of the saddest things I encountered were the historians who, for years, had been writing lies, who knew they were writing lies, but who now had to fess up. Some of them were very old, and they were smart, but now there was no longer any social ratification for what they had been doing. Their whole lives were a waste, and they knew it."

*In a secular age, the danger—the threat—is that you won't have any way of understanding what's more important than anything else when you're making decisions about how to go on.*
—Kelly

*On Sunday morning I went out for a while in the neighborhood and bought some raisin bread. The day was warm but a little sad, as Sundays often are*

*in Paris, especially when one doesn't*
*believe in God.*
—Houellebecq

*That state in which nothing seems more*
*important than anything else is what*
*Nietzsche called the state of nihilism;*
*every choice is equally good. Nietzsche*
*thought that was a great thing, but I*
*think we think that's an unlivable state*
*in which to find yourself.*
—Kelly

*Life is painful and disappointing. It is*
*useless, therefore, to write new realistic*
*novels. We generally know where we*
*stand in relation to reality and don't*
*care to know any more.*
—Houellebecq

*The academic study of literature leads*
*basically nowhere, as we all know.*
—Houellebecq

In an *Atlantic Monthly* cover article in 2014, Peter Pomerantsev, a USSR-born British journalist, called Surkov the "hidden author of Putinism":

*Surkov likes to invoke the new postmodern texts just translated into Russian, the breakdown of grand narratives, the impossibility of truth, how everything is only "simulacrum" and "simulacra," and then in the next moment he says how he despises relativism and loves conservatism, before quoting Allen Ginsberg's "Sunflower Sutra," in English and by heart.*
—Pomerantsev

*A real provocateur is someone who says things he doesn't think, just to shock.*
—Houellebecq

Usenet—User's Network—is a discussion system that's available by computer and distributed globally. In the early 1990s, when the internet become more widely available to consumers, James Parry, an inventor of digital typefaces and employee of world.std. com, an internet service provider, became known as the internet's biggest troll because he "grepped" Usenet for instances of the word *Kibo*, which he took as his nickname.

("Trolling" refers to the technique of dragging a lure from behind a fishing boat or dragging a fishing net along the bottom of the ocean floor. A "grep" is a computer command that's used to search plain-text data sets for lines that match a "regular expression." The meaning of *Kibo* is both "to shrug" and "to hope.")

Parry "grepped" Usenet for his nickname and would reply to every post that used it. Intending to cause confusion and offense, he would often insert non sequiturs into Usenet discussions, frequently targeting the Usenet discussion board for MENSA. In 1992, at age 25, he appeared on the cover of *Wired*, ran for president, and declared himself to be God.

> *I went back to* [Hannah] *Arendt's* Eichmann in Jerusalem *and reread sections of it. I was looking for a clue as to what she meant by "the banality of evil," which she defines as a "kind of thoughtlessness." I guess I think of evil as in some way connected with self-deception.*
> —Morris

> *Denialism has moved from the fringes to the center of public discourse, helped in part by new technology. As information becomes freer, as "research" has been opened to anyone with a web browser, as previously marginalized voices climb onto the online soapbox, so the opportunities for countering accepted truths multiply. No one can be entirely ostracized, marginalized, and dismissed as a crank anymore.*
> —Keith Kahn-Harris

*These are truly uncharted waters
for the country. We have in the past
argued over the values to be applied
to objective reality, or occasionally
over what constituted objective reality,
but never the existence or relevance of
objective reality itself.*
—Michael Hayden
(CIA director,
2018)

*We have a risk of getting to a place
where we don't have shared public
facts. A republic will not work if we
don't have shared facts.*
—Senator Ben Sasse
(Nebraska Republican,
2018)

Way, way, *way* too late.

In 1997, asked what he would say to the founding fathers, Gore Vidal said, "I'd say, 'Good try.'"

*Along with many other inventions
useful in the management of modern
states, the relatively new concept of*

*disinformation was recently imported
from Russia and is always openly
employed by a power—or by people
who hold a fragment of economic
or political authority—in order to
maintain what has already been
established and always in a counter-
offensive role. The confusionist concept
of disinformation is pushed into the
limelight to refute instantaneously—
by the very noise of its name—all
critique that has not been sufficiently
made to disappear by the diverse
agencies of the organization of silence.*
—Guy Debord (1988)

## Bannon

... So ... how did we get here?

One possibility is that someone smart on the right cribbed notes from the left and turned these notes against the left.

Or Steve Bannon and Stephen Miller came up with this stuff on their own; an alternative evolutionary species developed on the right....

Re: the early evolution of human beings, did we all evolve together, or did some hominids die out and others survive? Some theorists believe that all the hominids merged into homo sapiens; another school of thought argues that there were dozens of different hominids, several lines survived, and today we call all of them homo sapiens.

Did one hominid swallow all the others? E.g., did Bannon say, Hold the phone—I just figured out how to do this?

Maybe, though, all these people were just having their own conversations and developing their own alternative intellectual architecture—based on similar strategies—in the same way that early hominids did. An early hominid snuck over, saw the other tribe, ran back to his own tribe, and said, They have these tools; why don't we try to have similar or better tools?

Followers of Marine Le Pen are now reading Foucault.

There are, of course, American precedents for Trump: Jesse Ventura, Arnold Schwarzenegger, Ronald Reagan, George Romney, Teddy Roosevelt, Andrew Jackson. I can perform authoritarianism; elect me.

It's impossible to overemphasize the dialectic: without Obama, there is no Trump.

(And yet, of course, the contradictions ramify: After he was elected in 1992, Bill Clinton enacted welfare reform on a federal level, accomplishing in a single piece of legislation what Reagan had been attempting to do throughout the 1980s—requiring welfare recipients to work. In 2008, Obama, campaigning for president, said, "Ronald Reagan changed the trajectory of America. He tapped into what people were already feeling, which is: We want clarity; we want optimism; we want a return to that sense of entrepreneurship and dynamism that had been missing." In 2014, President Obama cut the nation's food stamp budget by eight billion dollars.)

A Black man and Black woman occupied the master suite of the White House: Fox News fanned the flames or just went ahead and started dumpster fires.

Enter Bannon. Harvard MBA. Hollywood producer. (His ten-year obsession: An adaptation of Shakespeare's play about the Roman general Titus Andronicus's return from war with four prisoners, who vow to take revenge against him; they rape and mutilate his daughter and have his sons banished and killed. Titus kills two of the prisoners and cooks them into a pie, which he serves to their mother before killing her, too.) Weirdly good on TV.

Attempting to defend his unintentionally myth-burnishing portrait of Bannon, *American Dharma*, Morris described Bannon as "intelligent, charming, and disarming in many, many, many ways."

There's only one rule: never be boring. Bannon isn't boring. (Biden is never not boring.) Bannon: I'm not going to wear one shirt untucked; I'm going to wear four shirts untucked and you won't be able to see where my belly begins and where it ends. The guy is fat as a whale. I'm Steve Fuckin' Bannon.

> *I'm a street fighter. That's what I am.*
> —Bannon

When the *Access Hollywood* tape was released, Trump went around the room and asked everyone what his chances of survival were. Zero. Zero. Zero. You're out. You're out. You're out. Bannon: You're 100% gonna win.

Trump: What should we do next? Bannon: Hold a rally, because you're Donald Trump, and they're not.

It's an old-fashioned cult of personality; it's a death cult.

It's not clear (and at this point it doesn't particularly matter) if Surkov explained to Bannon how disinformation works, or vice versa, because Trump revels in chaos, and most people don't; they will do anything to get the noise to stop. Asked how he handles the constant onslaught of the 24/7 media storm, Trump replied, "I *am* the storm."

> *I* am *the motherfuckin' shore patrol.*
> —Jack Nicholson,
> as Billy Buddusky,
> (in *The Last Detail*, 1973)

> *I use the word* rape *and all of a sudden everyone goes crazy.*
> —Trump

What does seem clear now is that Žižek, say, or Houellebecq turned twenty-two degrees to the right is Bannon.

> *The Democrats are not the opposition;*
> *the media is. . . . And the way to deal*
> *with* [the media] *is to flood the zone*
> *with shit.*
> —Bannon

In polls eight months before the 2024 election, Trump consistently led Biden in five key swing states by more than the margin of error. In one poll, Biden's approval rating was 39%; when Trump was president, his rating was never lower than 43%.

My former student Michael Sharick, who worked as an audio tech at Fox News Channel for many years, urged me to watch the "Fifteen Million Merits" episode of *Black Mirror*: "Most people spend all day every day on an exercise bike that generates energy. They live in 10 x10 cubicles with video screens for walls. Once in a while, a person can try out for an *American Idol*-style singing competition. If you do well, you might have other options in life beyond the bike. A man called Bing decides that the whole arrangement is unfair and infiltrates the audition. He hijacks the stage (and the cameras), holding a piece of sharp glass to his throat. Before the judges and a national audience, he threatens to kill himself if the government won't admit to its corruption. The judges take a moment, then applaud him, congratulating him on such an interesting new idea for a show. For a moment he looks stunned, but the next time we see him, he has a much nicer place to live, and he now spends most of his day in front of a camera, holding a piece of glass to his neck, yelling about government corruption."

According to Paul Piccone and Timothy Lake, former editors of the journal *Telos*, one of the consequences of late market capitalism is the advent of "artificial negativity," which poses as opposition to capitalism but only strengthens the dominance of the established system. The antiglobalization movement, the peace moment, the New Left, decolonization movements, and the environmental movement all serve to maintain the monopoly power of the state.

## Fake News

*One of the ways to have exciting new ideas is to tear everything to shreds and say everything was wrong, which was very welcome in many areas, because it undermined dedicated activism. The level of irrationality that grows out of this undermines the opportunity for doing something really significant and important.*
—Chomsky

*The people have been telling pollsters for decades that they want someone who is an outsider, a disrupter, an independent voice who doesn't owe anybody anything in Washington, and they finally got their wish with Donald J. Trump.*
—Kellyanne Conway

*One of [Trump's] first actions after taking the oath of office was to force his press secretary to tell a preposterous lie about the size of the inaugural crowd. The intention wasn't to deceive*

*anyone on the particular question of crowd size. The president sought to put the press and public on notice that he intended to bully his staff, bully the media, and bully the truth.*
—Jonathan Rauch

*You're saying it's a falsehood. Sean Spicer, our press secretary, gave alternative facts.*
—Conway

*A fact is an observation that has been repeatedly confirmed and for all practical purposes is accepted as true.*
—National Academy of Science

*Disagreement about core issues and even core facts is inherent in human nature and essential in a free society. If unanimity on core propositions is not possible or even desirable, what is necessary to have a functional social reality?*
—Rauch

*Now abideth beauty, truth, and intensity, but the greatest of these is intensity.*
—Houellebecq

*Playing hard is a talent.*
—George Karl
(retired NBA coach)

*The Democrats are playing beach volleyball. The Republicans are playing ice hockey.*
—Andrew Altschul

*Great counterpuncher. Donald Trump is a great counterpuncher.*
—Bannon

*Trump is getting away with literally everything. Very, very unusual.*
—Werner Herzog

*Cinema vérité is devoid of vérité. It reaches a merely superficial truth, the truth of accountants. One well-known representative of cinema vérité*

[Frederick Wiseman] *declared*
*publicly that truth can be easily*
*found by taking a camera and trying*
*to be honest. He resembles the night*
*watchman at the Supreme Court*
*who says, "There should be only one*
*law: the bad guys should go to jail."*
*Cinema vérité confounds fact and*
*truth and thus plows only stones.*
*Fact creates norms, and truth creates*
*illumination. There are deeper strata*
*of truth in cinema, and there is such*
*a thing as poetic, ecstatic truth. It is*
*mysterious and elusive and can be*
*reached only through fabrication and*
*imagination and stylization.*
—Herzog

*What you're seeing and what you're*
*reading is not what's happening.*
—Trump

*The current controversy over the*
*"post-fact era," "alternative facts,"*
*and "fake news" did not come*
*out of nowhere. Donald Trump,*
*Alex Jones, and Breitbart did not*
*materialize from the ether. Rather,*
*their prominence and success are the*
*outcome of decades of hard work*

*by denialists to encourage suspicion*
*toward scholarship and science.*
—Kahn-Harris

*No. You want it to be real. What I*
*want is the truth.*
—Conway

*I am the author, or one of the authors,*
*of the new Russian system.*
—Surkov

*There is really no fiction or nonfiction;*
*there is only narrative. One mode of*
*perception has no greater claim on the*
*truth than the other.*
—E.L. Doctorow

[In France] *we've had the National*
*Front for forty years, and it took*
*Trump only one year to get elected.*
*That's the surprising thing. In France,*
*we thought everybody liked Obama,*
*but maybe the media were lying.*
—Houellebecq

*An accusation that something is "fake news" seeks to be associated with striving to maintain truth, objectivity, and critical thinking, but the effect of its repeated use is to undermine those very values. This undermining has several mechanisms: allegations of fakery sap public trust in legitimate news institutions, and intellectual insults crowd out reasonable discourse.*
—Habgood-Coote

*Donald Trump has denied it, so I have no reason to believe otherwise.*
—Conway

*Denial hides from the truth. Denialism builds a new and better truth.*
—Kahn-Harris

*Trump is really a centrist liberal (in his economic policies, maybe even closer to the Democrats), and he desperately tries to mask this. The function of all his dirty jokes and stupidities is to cover up that he's really a pretty ordinary politician.*
—Žižek
(2016)

*You exist somewhere between your selves.*
—Surkov

*People quite often do not know what they want, or do not want what they know, or they simply want the wrong thing.*
—Žižek

*Boundless and overwhelming freedom always was and always will be pure political poison.*
—Surkov

*So long as man remains free, he strives for nothing so incessantly and so painfully as to find someone to worship.*
—Dostoevsky

*If you believe you are being constantly lied to, paradoxically you may be in danger of accepting the untruths of others.*
—Kahn-Harris

*Today, more and more in our public debate, we have this multicultural, multi-truth approach. The idea is that it's oppressive even to mention that sometimes there is one truth. The very culture of identity politics creates this kind of relativization where you are no longer able to criticize anyone. Instead of proposing an alternate vision of how to change things, all the left is doing, or at least what it's doing in the most convincing way, is making fun of Trump. All the big problems that we see today—the explosion of new populism, ecological disaster, and so on: Trump is the reaction. Trump is, as they say, an effect and not a cause. Fighting just Trump is what doctors call "symptomal healing."*
—Žižek

*Every single palm tree lining the entrance* [to Mar-a-Lago] *is like a masterpiece. Perfect height. True attention to detail.*
—Ivanka Trump, quoted on Trump's landscapers' website

*I'm like really smart.*
—Trump

*In 2017, when CNN fired three senior
journalists for getting a story wrong,
President Trump gloated that the
"Fake News" media's dishonesty had
been exposed. His tweet: "So they
caught Fake News CNN cold, but
what about NBC, CBS, & ABC?"*
—Rauch

*What* [Trump] *does on Twitter is
extraordinary. He disintermediates
the media.*
—Bannon

*Somebody said I'm the Ernest
Hemingway of 140 characters.*
—Trump

Possibly apocryphal, but the legend persists: In a Paris bar in 1923,
a friend bet Hemingway that he couldn't write a story in six words.
Supposedly, he came up with "For sale: baby shoes, never worn."

*I know words. I have the best words.*
—Trump

*I'm a very stable genius.*
—Trump

*It's a rigged election.*
—Trump

*My whole life is a fight. My whole life is
a fight. My whole life is a big fat fight.*
—Trump

*Life is warfare and a stranger's
sojourn, and after fame is oblivion.*
—Marcus Aurelius

*A Darwinian environment for ideas
is positive.*
—Bannon

*Big Tech and the Fake News Media
have partnered to Suppress. Freedom
of the Press is gone, a thing of the past.
That's why they refuse to report the real
facts and figures of the 2020 Election.*
—Trump

*We were getting ready to win this election. Frankly, we did win this election. This is a major fraud on our nation.*
—Trump

In November 2000, the Bush campaign staged what became known as the Brooks Brothers Riot: Bush campaign staffers stormed the facility in which election canvassers were recounting the votes for the presidential election. The aim of the demonstration was to disrupt the recount and ensure that the December 12 "safe harbor" deadline (after which no further objections could be filed) would pass without any further recount. After the riot—which, according to eyewitnesses, included "punching, trampling, and kicking"—the canvassing board unanimously voted to shut down for the day because the disruption had made the recount deadline impossible to meet.

In September 2020, the Aspen Institute—a nonprofit, progressive organization—held a "hack and leak" tabletop exercise and training session for executives from the *Washington Post*, Facebook, and many other media companies. The point of the exercise was to learn how to suppress Russian disinformation, with particular reference to information found on Hunter Biden's laptop. For at least a year the FBI had had the laptop in its possession and had already determined its authenticity.

On May 12, 2023, Special Prosecutor John H. Durham, whom Attorney General William Barr had appointed Special Counsel, released a report claiming that the FBI's "Crossfire Hurricane" investigation continued despite the intelligence community's awareness that there was no evidence of collusion between Trump and Russia.

> *I am the chosen one.*
> —Trump

> *I am a god.*
> —Kanye West

The chapter titles of Nietzsche's last book, *Ecce Homo: How One Becomes What One Is* (1888), are "Why I Am So Clever," "Why I Write Such Good Books, Part I," "Why I Write Such Good Books, Part II," "Why I Write Such Good Books, Part III," and "Why I Am a Destiny."

> *Man is weak, and when he makes*
> *strength his profession, he is weaker.*
> —Porchia

## Truth

*I have visited the laid-off factory
workers and the communities crushed
by our horrible and unfair trade
deals. These are the forgotten men and
women of our country: people who
work hard but no longer have a voice.
I AM YOUR VOICE.*
—Trump
(RNC acceptance speech, 2016)


*The truth has power. The truth will not
be threatened. The truth has a voice.*
—ubiquitous ad for the *New York
Times* (2016–2018)


*The cultural left increasingly
understands itself as a new
establishment of "power-knowledge,"
requiring piety and loyalty more than
accusation and critique.*
—Ross Douthat
(*NYT* columnist)

*The truth is essential. Life needs truth.*
—ad for *NYT*
(January 7, 2021)

*"Truth" is linked in circular relation*
*with systems of power that produce*
*and sustain it.*
—Geoffrey Shullenberger

*I know you think I'm interrupting*
*you, but I think the American people*
*deserve to have two or three minutes*
*of the truth.*
—Stephen Miller to Jake Tapper
on CNN

*Truth is relative.*
—Rudy Giuliani

*If a liar declares, "I am lying," is the*
*liar telling the truth?*
—Vittorio Bufacchi
(defining "liar's paradox")

*Trump's speaking style is from the future, from a time to come when human consciousness has broken down into floating splinters of subjectivity and superstition and jokes that aren't really jokes.*
—James Harper

*Some Americans believe that Elvis Presley is alive. Should we send him a Social Security check? Many people believe that vaccines cause autism or that Barack Obama was born in Africa or that the murder rate has risen. Who should decide who is right? And who should decide who gets to decide?*
—Rauch

*Social epistemology* [the evaluation of the social dimensions of knowledge or information] *is a fundamental problem for every culture and country, and the attempts to resolve it go back at least to Plato, who concluded that a philosopher king (presumably someone like Plato himself) should rule over reality.*
—Rauch

*Publishers Weekly* review of David Gress's *From Plato to NATO: The Idea of the West and Its Opponents* (1988): "Arguing that the US remains the bulwark and heartland of democratic liberal Western values, Gress mounts a withering attack on those he considers critics of modern capitalism and the West, including Sartre's slavish Stalinism, Toynbee's anti-Americanism, postmodernist nihilists, multiculturalists who assume that no single culture is preferable to any other, and 'Singapore school' economists who divorce economic development from political liberty."

*We demand to live in the world that*
*we imagine.*
—Richard B. Spencer
(alt-right neo-Nazi)

*Reality is what we know, not what*
*you or I know.*
—Rauch

[In 1967] *Arendt was already*
*lamenting the fact that politics and*
*truth don't mix, but even she was*
*aware that not all lies are the same.*
*There are lies that are minimal forms*
*of deception, a micro-tear in the*
*fabric of reality, while some lies are*
*so big that they require a complete*

*rearrangement of the whole factual
texture, a shift to another reality.*
—Bufacchi

*The visual has triumphed over the
literary, fragmented sound bites have
replaced linear thinking, nostalgia
has replaced historical consciousness,
simulacra are indistinguishable from
reality, an aesthetic of pastiche and
kitsch has replaced modernism's
striving for purity, and a shared
culture of vulgarity papers over
intensifying class disparities. In
virtually every detail, Trump seems
like the perfect manifestation of
postmodernism.*
—Jeet Heer

*The older, conservative critique of
relativism's corrosive spirit is still
largely correct. Which is why, even
when it lands telling blows against
progressive power, much of what
seems postmodern about the Trump-
era right also seems wicked, deceitful,
even devilish.*
—Douthat

*[The left's] abandonment of the tools
of critique offered by [Foucault's] work
has been sudden and almost total.*
—Shullenberger

*Maybe Putin and Trump's
postmodernist disdain for objective
facts is part of their appeal. Facts are,
after all, unpleasant things; they tell
you that you are going to die, that
you might not be good-looking, rich,
or clever. They remind you of your
limitations. There is a rebellious joy in
throwing off the weight of them.*
—Pomerantsev

Does "them" here refer to "limitations" or to "facts" or to both?

Does it matter, and if so, why?

## Dialectic

*Here ye strike but splintered hearts*
*together.*
—Melville

John Podhoretz, editor of *Commentary*, columnist for the *New York Post*, and former speechwriter for Reagan and Bush Sr., said, toward the end of Trump's presidency, "I don't know why he doesn't do a ninety-minute press conference three times a week. It wouldn't be good for the country but for his own ego and pleasure. He's never happier than when he's sparring with the press."

Whenever a "journalist" attempts to push back even slightly, Trump holds out his right hand like a stop sign and says, Excuse me, excuse me, excuse me—which means, I was talking (how dare you interrupt me), when all the person is trying to do is ask a question.

*Was George Washington a slave owner?*
*So will George Washington now lose*
*his status? Are we going to take down*
*statues to George Washington? How*
*about Thomas Jefferson?*
—Trump

*Until 150 years ago, slavery was*
*the rule. Slaveholding was common*
*among North American Indians.*
*Plato, Mohammed, and the Aztecs all*
*owned slaves.*
—Tucker Carlson

Trump will say, They're not the elite; we're the elite; we're better looking; we're richer; we have better houses; we're smarter. So now you can speak; I can speak; we can speak. Without the self-congratulatory censoriousness of the left, this maneuver wouldn't reverberate.

*In places like universities, where*
*everyone talks too rationally, it is*
*necessary for a kind of enchanter to*
*appear.*
—Joseph Beuys

Trump knows how to listen to his own, pseudo-Nietzschean nerve endings. He *feels* things and leans into them. It's extremely primitive.

*There's something deep in our*
*programming that says, "If a*
*homicidal alpha male shows up and*
*he's protecting my group, regardless*
*of what his other faults are, I've got*

*to follow him." That's very primal
programming. The demagogues—
whether it's Hitler or Milošević or
Trump—manipulate people so that
instead of being a German, you're an
Aryan; instead of being a Rwandan,
you're a Tutsi or Hutu; instead of
being a Yugoslav, you're a Serb or
Croat. Now it's our gene pool against
their gene pool. Trump and his people
just made it very explicit. Trump's
basic theme is, "I am the alpha male
of the white people. If you want to live,
follow me," and they did.*
—John Gartner

*One must be very naïve or dishonest to
imagine that men choose their beliefs
independently of their situation.*
—Lévi-Strauss

Rather like a patient undergoing psychoanalysis but mired in deep denial, Trump is terrified to experience his own suffering, which is what connects him to his followers. He shows them a way to stave off sadness.

Biden, of course, by contrast, has only one move: I, too, have suffered; am suffering; will continue to suffer. As if to explain to the quasi-sufferer what real suffering is, Putin quoted Tolstoy to Biden: "There is no happiness in life, only a mirage of it on the horizon."

Seventy percent of US GDP comes from blue states. It's no accident that Trump holds all his rallies in red states. He's an alternative opioid.

> We had fed the heart on fantasies, The
> heart's grown brutal from the fare;
> More substance in our enmities Than
> in our love ...
> —William Butler Yeats

What other person in the history of the world would spend twenty minutes attempting to explain that he wasn't really walking in a gingerly way down that ramp at West Point or would go on and on (apropos of nothing) about the existence/nonexistence of the "pee tape" or about how he has "big, beautiful hands," adding, "I'm fine down there"? He could hardly be conveying more clearly, I am (you are) a broken human being.

The story of the Garden of Eden isn't about morality; it's about finitude. The satanic figure of the serpent slithers in and asks, "Did God really say that? Did God really say that you're finite? Did God really say you can't eat from that tree?" Isn't that what Trump does? They say we can't get manufacturing back, etc. He denies

American finitude. He denies the reality that America is never going to get manufacturing back from China.

> *When the real is no longer what it was,*
> *nostalgia assumes its full meaning.*
> —Baudrillard

> [We] *will find the sacred and the gods*
> *that were there in these other epochs*
> *and bring them back in a new way.*
> —Dreyfus

Your son has died of an opioid overdose. The local medical genius
botched your wife's lap-band surgery. Your employer just shut-
tered its doors. Your daughter-in-law is on a ventilator from covid.
Reality is a nightmare. Who wants to deal with it? Bumper sticker:
GOD, GUNS, AND TRUMP. Lack and excess, baby.

> *Language isn't just a vehicle or a tool;*
> *it's the place where we meet.*
> —Robert Bly

On *Meet the Press*, Giuliani now said, with regard to Trump's testimony to the Mueller investigation, not just that truth is relative
but that "truth isn't truth." The left, or what passes for the left in
this country, responded by noting that there is now apparently

something called objective truth. Everywhere and always the *New York Times* runs an ad informing us that "The Truth Matters." What has happened?

> *Appearance and reality are not*
> *separated like oil and water in a vessel*
> *but rather are amalgamated like*
> *water and wine.*
> —Henri Lefebvre

—politics as nothing more or less than performance art:

After forty years of warning us about the dangers of postmodernism, the right now sounds like Jacques Derrida, and in the wake of Trump's kidnapping of Perspectivism, the left now sounds like Allan Bloom.

> *No one ever supposed that any one*
> *person had hold of it completely, but*
> *the goal was to seek the truth; the goal*
> *was the pursuit of truth.*
> —Cheney

> *The original is unfaithful to the*
> *translation.*
> —Jorge Luis Borges

(the law of unintended consequences)

We have no foundation, no floor, no ceiling. Either we retreat into a Bloomian Platonism, which is intellectually naïve and dead, or we give a Herzogian shrug and say, Stories are all we have and may the best story win, which is more or less a get-out-of-jail-free card for Trump, Putin, Surkov, Bannon, Bolsonaro, Erdoğan, Xi, Orbàn, Modi.

Trump gets that we like to see bad things happen to other human beings. This is terrible, but it's true.

> *The cruelty is the point.*
> —Adam Serwer

The clown Avner the Eccentric can easily walk straight between two trees on a slack rope, but for his act he lurches back and forth, mocks alarm, all but falls, and just barely makes it across. People dearly want him to fall. We will do anything to disrupt our lives. We worship chaos (from afar).

The Bible itself is, "unquestionably," a palimpsest of readings, misreadings, mistranslations, overwritings, pure conjecture, fiction, phantasm.

Norman Mailer's novel *Why Are We in Vietnam?*—published in 1967—mentions Vietnam only on the last page.

—the decline of the American empire.

> *Our capacity to live peaceably with*
> *each other depends upon our ability*
> *to converse intelligibly and reason*
> *coherently.*
> —Stout

—the end of Western civilization.

> *There are times when I catch myself*
> *believing there is something that is*
> *separate from something else.*
> —Bateson

—the search for truth understood, finally, as *the* human tragedy.

## Synopsis of Companion Film

At the NonfictioNow writers' conference in Phoenix on Nov 1–3, 2018 (a few days before the midterm elections), David Shields, Robin Hemley, and Nicole Walker asked their fellow writers and professors of nonfiction the following questions: *How do you know what you believe? Do you have any absolute beliefs? Is there such thing as "truth"? What is "nonfiction," and is it "true"? What do you think is the difference between "truth" and belief? If you have siblings, have they shown your view of the world to be flawed? Are you superstitious? Do you believe in ghosts? Why are you here and not canvassing for Stacey Abrams?*

The consensus answers: *I have no absolute beliefs except in art; there are no absolute truths other than that there is no truth; my sister and I are estranged; there are no ghosts except psychic luggage; I'm not canvassing for Abrams because all I finally care about is art.*

*How We Got Here* consists of interviews with more than thirty NonfictioNow attendees; eighteen brief 2-Truths-and-a-Lie videos, to demonstrate the precariousness of truth, especially now; and a slideshow / montage / soundscape / voiceover / monologue / rapid-fire intellectual history of the last 170 years.

## Early Praise for the Film

Official selection of the Golden State Film Festival, Culver City Film Festival, Marina del Rey Film Festival, and Indie Vegas Film Festival

"*How We Got Here* should be required viewing for every Intro to Humanities course in the country. It does the seemingly impossible: reinserts some context into our mostly decontextualized lives. And, perhaps even more surprisingly, the film's pace and structure prevent it from ever feeling even slightly boring, despite the heavy lifting it does to excavate the ideological roots beneath our country's growing social and political turmoil." — Michael Wheaton, *Autofocus*

"A brilliant, encyclopedic film, about the history of the idea of truth. The meanings are conveyed by how the film is edited: the quick cutting, the arrangement of quotations, the personal versions articulated by different speakers, the black-and-white live action, the color animation, and the intersplicing of Two Truths and a Lie videos."—Susan Daitch, author of *Siege of Comedians: A Novel*

"A fast-paced, exhilarating collage of voices converging on the question of how we got to birtherism and election denial."—Jennifer Jacquet, author of *The Playbook: How to Deny Science, Sell Lies, and Make a Killing in the Corporate World*

## Digital Links to Film

Link to film on Prime Video:
https://www.amazon.com/How-Got-Here-Elena-Passarello/
dp/B0CX5NTBKQ

(also streaming on Tubi, Roku, Cineverse, OTT Studio, and Future Today)

Film trailer:
https://www.how-we-got-here-film.com/trailer

Silent video loop:
https://vimeo.com/755817023

Film poster:
https://drive.google.com/file/d/1wkjQlfi8U5aj_8C5mNGnka-Zvl-tFNmuJ/view?usp=drive_link

Film website:
https://www.how-we-got-here-film.com/

## About the Author

David Shields is the internationally bestselling author of twenty-five books, including *Reality Hunger* (which, in 2020, *Lit Hub* named one of the most important books of the past decade), *The Thing About Life Is That One Day You'll Be Dead* (*New York Times* bestseller), *Black Planet: Facing Race During an NBA Season* (finalist for the National Book Critics Circle Award and PEN USA Award), *Remote: Reflections on Life in the Shadow of Celebrity* (PEN/Revson Award), and *Other People: Takes & Mistakes* (*NYTBR* Editors' Choice). *The Very Last Interview* was published by New York Review Books in 2022.

The recipient of a Guggenheim fellowship, two NEA fellowships, and a New York Foundation for the Arts fellowship, Shields—a senior contributing editor of *Conjunctions*—has published essays and stories in *New York Times Magazine, Harper's, Esquire, Yale Review, Salon, Slate, Tin House, A Public Space, McSweeney's, Believer, HuffPost, Los Angeles Review of Books,* and *Best American Essays.* His work has been translated into two dozen languages.

The film adaptation of *I Think You're Totally Wrong: A Quarrel,* which Shields co-wrote and co-stars in, was released in 2017 (available now as a DVD on Prime). Shields wrote, produced, and directed *Lynch: A History,* a 2019 documentary about Marshawn Lynch's use of silence, echo, and mimicry as key tools of resistance (streaming on Prime, Peacock, AMC, Sundance, Apple, and several other platforms).

*I'll Show You Mine*, a 2023 feature film that Shields co-wrote and was produced by Mark and Jay Duplass, is streaming on Prime and other platforms.

Printed in the USA
CPSIA information can be obtained
at www.ICGtesting.com
JSHW081048260524
63600JS00001B/14